STRICTLY NO POETRY

STRICTLY NO POETRY

AIDAN MATHEWS

THE LILLIPUT PRESS
DUBLIN

First published 2018 by
THE LILLIPUT PRESS
62–63 Sitric Road, Arbour Hill
Dublin 7, Ireland
www.lilliputpress.ie

ISBN 978 1 84351 744 3

A CIP record for this title is available
from The British Library.

1 3 5 7 9 10 8 6 4 2

Set in 11.5 pt on 18 pt Quixote by Marsha Swan
Printed in Spain by GraphyCems

For G – in a different day of the week, a different season,
the same vigil of Advent

Contents

STRICTLY NO POETRY

AMDG

Chalk on a classroom slate
Kick-started the process:
Capital letters mating
In a stick insect cursive
In the shadow of Mother Power,
Now Vera, a centenarian
Astray in the convent parlour
And staring at an aquarium.

From the nights of diary entries
In the Ancient Greek alphabet
Of the strange seminal ventures
My mother failed to interpret;
To the pages my daughters proofread
To protect me from myself
And to keep my high and my low-grade
Shelf life above sea level.

From the cut-and-thrust of Querty
To the cut-and-paste of Apple,
From the holiness of dirt

To the sanctity of debacles
When it hurts to write in longhand –
No flick of the wrist for physios –
But I persevere in my plan
Which is G minor *con brio*.

I wrote about Death and Time.
Now it's sex and alcohol,
And a troll's slow-motion rhymes
Of the All with the Individual.
Microsoft Windows next stop.
Yet the arrow and the hourglass
Hover still here on the desktop
To honour the lovely impasse

As my first imperial purple
Flow pen in olden schooldays.
Open my lips again. I will marvel.
I will marvel out loud and praise
Worlds and their wives' entreaties
To the ladychapel's Lord,
The margin ruled with AMDG,
My first four-letter word.

AFTER OMAGH

It was where you turn at the meat processing plant.
I braked for ambulances, police panda cars,
But what exploded there out of the silent cinema
Was a nineteen-twenties vintage model Ford;
A Brylcreemed bridegroom and his Gatsby bride;
Her veil in the vents of the wind like a first-aid dressing,
And the wedding convoy's horns.

They were the treble of school bells, falsetto all clears,
The baritone of wild geese from their arctic detour,
Nude picture postcards in an alarmed letterbox;
And they were the howl of the grounds of a great
    house closing,
The uproar of the primates in the zoo at nightfall,
Or the office fire drill where I file in shirtsleeves
And the steward lists the missing.

I leaned on my own car horn until my palm hurt,
Pressing it like the one note of an accordion
In my soundproofed Southern car. The rest is sirens ...
They will leave the queer mirrors of their hotel elevator
To watch the wedding video with the volume turned
    down;

And the soprano in the News for the Deaf at midnight
Will be dumbfounded too at their shapes under a sheet.

AT THE JUNCTION

There is the hum of car windows closing.
Even the sunroofs slip shut with a sigh
As refugees at the red light infiltrate
The lane discipline of our stalled drive time.

Some brat of an Indo-European lavishes
Lather on my own clean windscreen.
The wipers stop, stuck in the slush,
Like the wartime whitewashed windowpanes

Of a tram that crossed through the Warsaw ghetto.
But I won't be blackmailed by sob stories,
I who drive an economy Opel
From outpatients to outpatients,

A middle-aged manic-depressive male
Whose gifts at the altar are all
Wafer-thin, watered down, tactical;
And who hardly remembers the time or the day

When Masahiko from Tokyo came
To a Cabinteely cul-de-sac
And the children there queued up in a line

To stroke his goatee beard like a bell rope,

Its sleek silvery Shinto softness
Shining and winding its way down
To where I could see the paw prints of infants,
A moon looming over a hangnail.

ANN

Her coffin lid ajar for our gifts in the oratory
Was like a parcel packed for an orphan in Eastern Europe
With its little useless, wrapped non-perishables:
Beads and a bear and the curled family photographs
That had bleached to albinos almost on the white sill of
    a window.
Thus the Christmas box for the ruined Muslim villages.

Stowing a shoebox then with its greetings to Kosovo
Guided me back to her bedside in the hospice:
The rosary, the koala, the plastic bib that she wore,
Foetal and sleepy among the dark monitors,
With her two still hands that had knitted together such
Balaclavas and mittens for the Red Cross mercy missions.

DECENCY

Granny's smoking in her sickroom
On the left-hand side of the landing.
Life goes so fast. She can't draw breath.
If I knock at her door she'll be squatting
On a jumbo bale of geriatric diapers.

On the right-hand side of the landing,
The lovely scent of my daughter's urine.
I butter her vulva with cold cream,
Her scorched anus, her dimply bum,
And I parcel her into a sellotaped Pampers.

In the middle, straight before me,
At eye level, my level, a tacked crucifix.
Jesus in a loincloth on the cross.
What I wondered at fifteen was:
Were they ashamed to show his cock?

Had his cadaver a hard-on?
Was the Church ashamed he'd been docked,
A Jew of the House of Jacob,
Or was it, as the Schoolmen argued,
That he had never defecated?

You live. You learn. Life goes so fast.
Whether swaddling clothes in a stable
Or a linen sheet in the tomb,
There are things so holy they should be hidden –
Those parts of the body that moisten

To disclose fully the flesh and blood
Which haunts us more than metaphysics.
It is our own species we eat and drink
And the odour of sanctity on my hands –
Shit and piss – is a relic of decency.

EMILY'S MEMORY

Emily's millennium was no milestone,
Several months short of the scheduled street carnival.

Yet it still stopped city-centre traffic
In its tracks, a red flicker at the heart of gridlock.

She was almost ninety-five. She was well beyond it.
In her lilac studio loft with its Easter lilies

British militia once filed past a milliner
Who has morphed now into mobile phones,
   stretch limos,

A Pope abolishing limbo. There is no end to it.
She befriended the solid floor of the world:

Limestone, linoleum, Tintawn, tiles of parquet.
It shakes still to her mild and wilful foot sole

And the cry of an adult calling her name today
To a Laura Ashley child at the invalid parking space.

HEALING THE LEPERS

Not like Flaubert's Saint Julian, avid for display
And condescending from camelback in an
   Eastern chasuble –
Let us say it was the feast of Corpus Christi –
To kiss a leper once, his lips' peeled rubber,
And ride off then spectacularly into the encyclicals
As the touched man turned to Jesus in a dust cloud
And the dust cloud lifted for the stones to hurtle.

But more a matter of Damian, Father Damian say,
With his discount antiseptics, his stamp-sized
   missal pictures,
Lying down with that leper there and kissing her lips
Wherever it was possible for him to do so,
No emissary with caresses but a partner;
And lifting local breadloaf, a rotgut rosé wine,
His hands unwinding like the wool of a stigmatist's
   mittens.

For two years in the hush of a mental hospital
A third man cried in a corner, cigarette ash on his slippers,
But made it back at last to the world of water sprinklers.

Now the social lepers lurch in their own light towards
    him,
Damaged and ageing. They are as human as God.
And he must wipe their feet with his Holy Communion
    jumper
And warm the chilblained stumps in a tub of his urine.

SOUND EFFECTS IN A STUDIO

The actors drinking wine on microphone
Are drinking water only.
Their cut glass is cracked Styrofoam.

My eighteenth-century heroine
Faints in a tank top
And warm leggings under a denim mini

Unlike the World Service announcers
In shot silk and satin dresses
Who once introduced operas,

Curtain calls across static Europe.
She is more like a Greek station porter
With his left luggage and lost luggage

Who is called *Kurios Metaphor*.
So let one thing stand for another.
Let us walk on sacred ground

By twisting cotton wool for snowshoes.
Let it rain dry rice in a jam jar.
Let the creak of our stolen currach

Be buttocks on a leatherette bar stool;
Our kisses a lip-smacked wrist
And the radio studio a radiant study

Or a bedroom, even, where two sweethearts
Are sound asleep in real linen. They could be
You and me if the red light were off:

Your breathing through a blocked nose now
A breeze on the face of the deep,
My silence the only word for it.

KYRIE FOR A COUNSELLOR

i.m. Cearbhall O Dálaigh

The acapella of wolves
Is what I recall, the long low
Solo of the orangutan
And the Greek Orthodox baritone
Of the bull elephant in his pen.
What keys can unlock them now?

It is two in the morning, so,
In the fierce middle of Dublin,
All my two children ago.
I am typing on an Underwood
Your note of resignation,
Your last wistful aria.

Recitative of flamingoes
Italicizes the darkness,
A rush of silver lances;
And the toothless MGM lion
Rattles the railings of his cage
Like the warm gusts in the Underground.

Without training, without Typex,

I type it out *ad nauseam*:
The same six wry sentences
On the big embossed stationery,
One Rothmans per revision
As if it were almost a poem,

A death haiku, a love cry,
A genealogical litany
Of the *dáileach*, the counsellor,
Cearbhall, the giver of torcs,
My Charlie Chaplin godfather,
A *padrino*, no *padrone*,

With his Pentecostal tongue –
Irish, French, High German,
Italian and Esperanto –
Housecarl, *primus inter pares*.
In your kitchen in the small hours
Foxes drank from the cat's saucer.

Once at a public swimming pool
You undressed before me, disrobed
To the stencils of your socks
On your slender Achilles' heels.
I saw your beautiful nakedness:

The boy's wrists, the baby pubis.

And once in a Botticelli brochure,
Browsing for breasts and bottoms,
I found the Prisons' Maintenance Act
With your annotated account of one
Procedural supervised flogging
In the year of the dog and Yuri Gagarin

As if you were trying to tell me
That the Paraclete must come down
To cleanse the Augean stables
Of the criminal justice system
That you hated and held accountable
To our crucified, liminal Godman.

Such keening and lamentation
From the Zoological Gardens
Where you carried me on your shoulders
To watch the sea lions caper
Who would change their shapes at midnight
To dowagers, debutantes, girls

And a Greek chorus of androgynes
In the Delphic silver of church bells,

Stepping out of their pelts
As the paper spills from my carriage,
Streaked and ghastly and crumpled,
With the saline odour of howls.

LAST THINGS

When Wittgenstein's cottage in Galway was unlocked
He had outwitted his critics: thousands of comics

Rose up among mice droppings where they had wanted
To find folios from an *übermensch*, not *Superman*.

And Yeats, dying so intently on the Côte d'Azur,
Read Westerns while he worked on his obituary

Though lariats turn to cinctures in the last verses.
Cú Chulainn was present, but also Bat Masterson.

Which is to say we aim at shoddy rapture.
The trash of dailiness has warmed us like newspaper

Down through the years inside our vests and jackets
Against all weathers. When we must manage naked,

Some sheet of it may seem less print than parchment
From the event of its being bodily sheltered

As if the humdrum could become papyrus
Because we had touched it and held it close to us,
The breastplate of the tramp, the thing that lasts.

MAGDALENES

On a weekend with my child in her Cambridge college
Don't I go and call Magdalen 'Magdalene' in a blunder
Same as the laundry back in Donnybrook village
Where the parrot knew the start of the Hail Mary
In the best Church Latin as far as *Dominus tecum?*
When I put the Dublin *the* in front of *Magnificat*
The punters smile at my gaffe like the Dalai Lama.

Then, for a moment, I whiten to shorts and school cap
Beside myself at the troughs where the washerwomen
Stab at our dirty linen with white bamboo poles:
The Y-fronts auburn with turd, pyjamas silver with semen,
And the drift of my father's cotton detachable collars
That he wore like stocks in the witness box in the
    Four Courts
In the course of his own, his medico-legal, maudlin.

MERCY, CHARITY

Small talk. Big talk. Talk about the medium.
In the reward-winning documentary unit
A ginger group is getting galvanized
Among spider plants that have died for want of being
    watered,
About the Middle Ages, the Magdalene bondage,
The lamb and the shambles and the fallen same old,
    same old.

You can still see them, Charity and Mercy,
Old women walking together, arm in arm, actually,
All sisters now, annulled, the unveiled olden inmates
And the mothers inferior in their barefoot lockstep.
It is hard to tell where they shuffle which is which
As they wend their way, as they cross from right to wrong,
Between the important brass of the choked motorway
And the woodwind of the tennis club's pavilion
Where the ball would be thrown back
Sometimes, an odd time, over the convent wall,
Its eglantine and birdsong and fanged bottle ends,
To roll like a card of green wool, a clue of sorts,
In the long evenings, in the lengthening shade,
To my very own sneakered footfall, the whitewashed heel,

Of a twelve-year-old who came second in each set
On every kind of court, grass, gravel or clay,
Like the three stages of a grave as the gradual
Heart revives in its hard happiness.

Tonight in the documentary unit
Between the commercial break and the next Nicorette
    patch
The thirty-somethings brighten at the hostess trolley
Pushed punctually by a girl from Burkina Faso
Whose two children are being raised by her own
    grandmother,
And whose outlawed in-laws in the internment camp,
A barbed-wire Billy Butlin's just north of here now,
Must wait for forty years, presumably, in the deserted
Foreseeable future for our children's children's
Small talk; for their big talk; for their talk of the media,

A medium that may also mean a séance,
A table-thumping, clever ventriloquial voices,
Almost immediately after, a keystroke, a carriage-flick
    further,
In the online, scrolled-down silence of Wikipedia.

GRANDFATHER

A pest of a poor dad made my best grandfather,
The whiskey priest who guested as patron saint

When my own *paterfamilias* was neither
Paternal/familiar. Yet my mum, his daughter,
   shunned him

As he scrunched the gravel drive at the granite gate,
The closest she'd ever come to gritty realism

That sound of bespoke shoes which tapped accelerators
In time to the rhythm and blues of Radio Caroline,

The steps that stopped. He'd be bowing to the
   snowdrops,
A cabin boy again at the tradesman's entrance.

I realize that your death transformed you utterly,
Your nineteen lives, out of all our recognitions,

The way that a solitary spermatozoon
Egged on by the Holy Spirit of God Almighty

May soar to the future stature of a Michelangelo,
Maybe, or even an Amadeus, *mar dhea*,

In the fullness of the time that takes up all eternity.
It's in Corinthians. Eye hath not seen, *et cetera* –

Your sclera saffron like a smoker's fingernail
And your dentures loose with laughter from my trick
    fart cushion –

How we are changed, exchanged, hidden, made manifest:
Our cling-film form a sudden cut-glass goblet,

Waterford crystal-like, with no whiff of Courvoisier.
But I loved you as you were, for richer, for poorer,

Your eyebrows box-hedged at breakfast time with a
    toothbrush,
Your ear a map of old Magellan's Africa,

And your bird-of-paradise tie thrown back triumphantly
Over the giant shoulder like an antimacassar

Or the battle standard of a standard-bearer
For your first second helping of an oxtail casserole.

COVENANT OF THE OVEN

In a camp surrounded by Christmas trees
Where my mother would have draped threads of lametta –
The politely Italian old-German word for *razor blade* –
On the non-shedding variety

There was a chimney in which every Santa letter
Went awol finally from the bipolar planet,
Enveloped in a pillar of smoke during office hours,
In a pillar of fire at the lighting of candles.

DOING TIME

On my first day in prep school
In 1964 AD
A man in the college blazer,
A sixth year with blonde sideburns,
Asks me to sign a petition
For release from an African prison
Of a person called Nelson Mandela.
'Have you the time?' he wants to know
And I show him my whistling Swiss watch
From my Holy Communion cash flow
As the handbell rings for class.

I grow up, I go to university
Where, for the time being,
I study clockwork, chronology,
The arrow of time itself
That is life-giving and lethal,
And marvel at the Eternal.
I have, in fact, the time of my life:
Eschatological time,
Existential time,
Proust's time, Bergson's time,
Memory and amnesia,

Endurance and duration,
The womanly curve of Einstein's time,
And in no time at all,
The punctual girl with the hourglass pelvis
Under the clock in the library apse
Who has slipped off her espadrilles
To smoke a Gold Bond on the stroke of twelve
As a seminarian stands for the Angelus.

I spend ten swift years at three such
Slow, time-honoured institutions,
Each with its ivied campanile,
Each with its timeless chimes,
Until, in the fullness of time, I find
There is no more time to lose.
It's a job or the dole. I am interviewed.

On my first day on a convent school staff
In 1984 AD
A blonde schoolgirl picks at my jacket
As the buzzer rings for classes
And she says to me: 'Have you time, sir,
To sign a petition for a prisoner in jail,
An African called Nelson Mandela?'

PERPETUAL OUTING

First Mellifont, then Mosney.
From the strict Cistercian cloister
Where an otter frisked in the baptistery
In contempt of the Drogheda beagle
To the Holy Ghost chaplain in Butlin's
At the deep end of the swimming pool
Who showed us our first Frisbee;
And ending up in St Peter's
At the head of Oliver Plunkett
In its Pye-radio reliquary,
A ball of beeswax behind bulletproof glass,
A long-wave whisper.

It all boomerangs back.
That was the old itinerary,
The family outing in my father's automatic,
Sunday after Sunday after Sunday afternoon
From Eastertide to August, a summertime
Tour of the twentieth century's dusking
From the last tulip to the first windfall
With the sun in our eyes like a cine projector bulb
All the way home again, home.

Now the handcuffed clerics on the plasma screen
Scowl in slow motion. It is monochrome.
The new convent at Collen looks like a Lager.
In the holiday camp with the hum of its sensor system
Black men that were blue men in our crucified classroom
Bleach to the kitchen likeness on the Trócaire box.
Their pocket money each seventh day's advent
The price of a parking ticket for sixty minutes
In the underground Abbey Theatre car park
That smells like a nuclear bunker now
With a slipstream of Chanel in the elevator.

Which is where I have found my father's Mercedes,
RZE 220, with a vintage/veteran sticker
From a Patrick's Day parade in a place called Oughterard,
With the scuff marks on the elbow rests and ashtrays
Where dachshund after dachshund, all called Scamp,
Who had bitten at more than they could chew,
Scrabbled with their paws and soiled the padding
Of their own particular ramp
Before being put to sleep by lethal injection.

MURALS
for Gerry Dawe

Just as you can drive in South Dublin
To a Falls Road in the heart of a Shankill,
And idle there, listening to Lyric FM –
Haydn, say, who scored for both sides,
Catholic and Protestant, blithely;
So too you can fantasize *al fresco*
About those rival murals back in Belfast.
Hearsay has it the same artist
Who gave us King Billy on a broodmare
At the gable end of one perished postcode
Brush-stroked Bobby Sands' brown hair too
On a terracotta breeze block downtown.
If the writing's ever on the wall,
That's it, must be: an interlinear script
To hint at the red-handed ambidexterity
Of an artisan Irishman dreaming in 3-D
A freestyle, non-terrestrial station.

Fall on your platinum kneecap on the green
Astroturf of the squash-courts that were chancels,
And inhale it like hash, the pubic whiff
Of potpourri and aerosol spray cans.

That orange behind your eye is a sunspot
Lighting up Carson's temple as it throbs
In the indigo lap of the Blessed Virgin
While Pearse picks sugar lumps from his holster
For the biddable Williamite charger
On the Arts Council catalogue jacket.
We laminate in limited editions
Our site-specific, street-theatre tragedies,
And put our faith in intercultural pleas –
All atheists, all ecumenists, we –
Quitting the bloody-minded bread and wine
At last for the bloodless wine and cheese.

THE FINAL SOLUTION

Delos, for three centuries
An Asian Minor marketplace
For slaves and the subhuman.
Millions had passed that way.
We did it in a day
From the gay island of Mykonos
That we'd tired of temporarily,
All kaftans and rave vocals.

What I remember most
Were the lizards sidling swiftly
In the theatre like a fingerprint
Where Euripides had played
To the Greek *Untersturmführers*
Weighing breasts and testicles.
Their swish in the grass made you wet
Your disposable paper panties.

Barbados was the next.
It took a fluke of weather,
The sand going grey in the face
Under rainclouds and gusting
Sea squalls to gather all

The holidaymakers together –
Their sunblock, their ghost bikinis! –
In the modest new museum

Where the nipple-to-nipple brand –
SPCK in reverse –
Was the eighteenth-century logo
Of a London Bible society
For promotion of Christian knowledge,
And where Thomas Thistlethwaite liked
To shit in his classical colonnade
For a slave of the stool to panhandle.

Auschwitz will be the same.
Our children will live to see it.
A golf-course architect mapping
The eighteenth hole at a bunker
Where the sand is burnt *homo sapiens*;
Or elderly naturists walking
On the tips of their toes through the pine trees
With their shoes and socks in their hands.

PHRASES
i.m. Mairín O Dálaigh

There was something that you hummed
Only when you were happy,
Preserving fruit in the pantry
Or writing the whole of the letter C
(Three volumes) for an Old Irish dictionary.

It was the same when you bathed me
With your red kitchen gloves
And my palms over my nipples;
Or in among the beehives –
Such humming from the helmeted memsahib.

No one living recalls it at all,
The old Protestant neighbour
Or me whom you dressed and undressed.
It's gone like the sore ovaries
Of a girl scrubbing floors in Pompeii,

The Delphic oracle's apricot skin
Or the plyboard plaque that read
Jesus of Nazareth, King of the Jews
In three dead languages.

Once in the middle of the night

The gist of it gifted my listening.
I went downstairs in the dark, all ears,
To search for a Sony cassette recorder;
But the phrase swerved in my mouth to a mix
Of offertory hymn and three-chord pop tune.

When my daughter learns words like *caínt*
Or *cómhrá*, I think of your hard slog –
Thirty years serving and preserving;
Or a TV programme on beekeeping
Will hum in the same unison and harmony.

Maybe God the Father or God the Son
Will greet me with it, a dog's whistle.
Maybe it was bar twenty-four to bar thirty
Of some heavenly chorus
The Holy Spirit would sing if she had the air.

THE STATE OF THE CHURCH

A bird's building I don't know what
On the old overspill loudspeaker
At the west door with the new wheelchair ramp.

Inside in the left confessional
The parish hygiene committee has stored
The mobile font and a Nilfisk vacuum cleaner.

Pews that were sold will probably surface
In an LGBT pub soon. And those marble
Altar rails with the trailing stone grapes

Will trellis a heated swimming pool
Where the kids at the deep end dive to the green
Tiling to pee, to peer up at legs

In a swaying Sistine Chapel above them.
Already women are out buying Chilean
Wine for the family table; already

Inmates of John of God Hospital
Are baking scones for their tranquillized wives
In the Occupational Therapy ovens.

Pray silence so. They will be reading lessons,
Telling stories, giving thanks together,
Sharing food and pouring plonk as if

Jesus the Jew were really present there.
Not one of them's been to Mass for ages.
Not one of them has the least idea

What the true church of the state is today.
Look at weddings and funerals, for God's sake:
Sitting down when they should stand up,

Standing up when they should kneel,
As if it were up to the weeks of February
And March to heal the face of the frozen earth.

THE BERLIN WALL

I came home from hospital to find the Wall fallen.
It was two years later. Like that prisoner-of-war old
   Gerhart
Walking home from the Ukraine the year I was born
To his whiskered mother at the border, with a photograph
Of a smiling adolescent in her hatband,
My feet hummed from the metalled roads. You were
   much older.

Cream for your crow's feet on the dressing table.
I walked our baby round and round in the searchlight
Of the television set. Men and women were scattering
The writing on the Wall, the beautiful spray-can frescoes.
Her drool on my shoulder glittered like epaulettes.
The earthen smell of her bum purified the temple.

When there was war between the parents, rare wildflowers
Flourished among those landmines. Herons colonized
The one hundred metres between pillbox and bunker.
Ornithologists from all over climbed the watchtowers
With Army binoculars that had night vision.
The two of us prayed in a ward without moving our faces.

Her weight on my shoulder felt like a small stroke.

Diapers stirred on the line. They were flags of truce.

Hands reached through concrete holes and chanced
    their arms.

I would have woken you. I had lost that freedom.

The tremor in my hands was not medication.

It was the psalm of my body. It was the future passing.

That was three in the morning. I danced with a vomiting
    infant

Like a scroll of the Torah. Her mother dreamed it upstairs

In a Zimovane vision, in the deep sleep of the just.

I thought of a schoolfriend's father whose incendiary
    bombs

Cremated the kindergartens, and who went back

Two years later in the same Lancaster with ton after ton
    of water.

THE DEATH OF TED HUGHES

Word on the wireless was how we heard. I was gouging
    a pumpkin –
Arrowheads for the eye sockets, harrow teeth for a smile
And a nightlight loaned from the shrine of Our Lady
    of Sorrows.

I could see through my windowed image trepanning
    the skullcap
The ghosts of the shipwrecked indoors astray on our
    washing line,
My ornamental fruit trees demented by forest.

There was the smell of smoke, of turf smoke and
    woodsmoke,
Of bonfires in the field with the headlamps of squad cars,
And smoke on my golden fingernails, smoke in my
    fillings.

Breath from the breathing dead on the eve of All Hallows
Clouded the little depression in which I live.
There were so many dead around me in those blurred
    brown terraces –

Thousands and still thousands, not counting women
    or children,
A phantom encampment, the pilgrim millions – I went
    and made up
Pet names for our great-grandparents humming

Travellers like us to sleep through Istanbul,
Constantinople and Byzantium and Miklagard;
And I put out heels and mackerel for the pagan Jesus

To take and bless and break and pass them round
From the big black baskets stacked at the door for
    burning,
To the quiet, feeding multitudes who are more than we
    know now.

THE ELEMENTS OF LEAVING
for G, an emigrant

From the ruined chancel at Rathmichael
You lined your foot soles with old topsoil.

I was in flip-flops. It was your walkabout.

The Poulaphouca reservoir
Poured pure Wicklow water into a Lourdes bottle.

Now it's in Melbourne. It's entirely elsewhere.

After that birthday candle in Cabinteely
Your lighter won't strike fire again until Australia,

Heavy as any hearthstone in your breast pocket.

Over the terracotta rooftops of Kilmacud
Helium filled the farewell novelty condoms.

Your wine breath gushed from one that wouldn't knot.

IMPERIAL WAR MUSEUM

Watching a war film with you
A week before you die,
I remember only embarrassment
The time you lifted me down
Inside a Spitfire's cockpit
As an ex-serviceman smiled.

At the military parade
For the 1916 Rising,
Spitfires stooped on O'Connell Street.
I held onto your sleeve among
Veterans' urinous trouserlegs,
Lapels with metal tricolours.

While you were performing maybe
A corporectomy, was it,
I glued a Spitfire together
From a plastic skeleton kit
And landed it on your bureau.
That won't get you into college,

To Biggin Hill or Biggles.
How many bones in the hand?

How many hands in the pot?
Make a fist of your hand while you can!
But now your finger is shaking
Like a boy's touching a breast

As you point at the battle of Britain
On the set with too many ad breaks
Full of beautiful, healing flesh.
So many minor strokes
Have made you half-human again,
Have brought you down to earth

Like the paralyzed man in Luke
Let down through the roof by his friends,
No *deus ex machina*
But a crash-landed pilot
Where the ground gives and forgives
And a parachute lags the immersion.

When you die I will kiss your hand
On its heavy, hardened palm
Where you started a stopped heart
In the operating theatre
Or groomed the underarm hairs
Of the woman I knew as my mother.

Yet watching the war film with you
Something in us has been heightened –
A wing and a prayer in English,
The flight of father and son –
As I try to talk you down
On your sky-blue final throne.

THE WESTERN TRADITION

Aristotle's slogan stands over Auschwitz:
Arbeit macht frei. The work shall set you free.
But it is Plato's motto that fits the statistics:
Let no one without mathematics enter me.

VERGES

A fish out of water, the old German Jesuit
Who survived the atom bomb at Hiroshima
Would cross the main Sandford road at rush hour
Without once glancing up from his black breviary.

He was radioactive still. Transistor
Static crackled from his tortoise-shell spectacles
While he walked as if he were working a treadle,
Slow-motion skips. A late sickness. The last stroke.

No schoolboy ever spoke to him. Otto
Scarface Skorzeny SS lived locally
Who had spirited Mussolini from a prison cell
To the Führer's white fortress at Berchtesgaden;

And General Mulcahy's grandson sat beside me
In the odour of classroom maps that had altered
Each decade for a century with the start of more talks
About borders bordering on the ridiculous.

Seventy-seven death warrants signed
By the old martial lawyer kneeling at morning Mass
A pupil could zero in on more than on light

Spray painting the kimono stencils of the vanished.

But when the garden fete at Milltown Park
Ended with Benediction, that Jesuit cripple
Back-pedalled along the avenue to wherever
Goldfish in plastic bags had been thrown from cars.

He carried them like bullion in his arms –
As the sun set on the land of the rising moon –
Against the convoys, and he slipped them one by one
Into the priests' pond in the Japanese garden.

PARISH CURATE 2020

Dead of night. Off the new EU bypass
A cattle grid, a gravel drive, a gnome;
Halogen glare of the terrified porch sensor.
On the gable of a Type-B bungalow
Over the last man's lead-frame bay window,
A satellite dish like a begging bowl
Fills with the fish scales of old starlight.

Nunc dimittis servum tuum, Domine,
Secundum verbum tuum in pace.

His voicemail message is in ansa mode.
Speak at the chirpy cheep. And he lies there
Lengthwise on a leatherette two-seater
Sofa, dozing, his squash-court elbow tilted.
The smoking finger points like a teapot putto
To a sea-shell ashtray, a Tayto sandwich,
Cold pizza wolfed in its Tudor cardboard box.

Quia viderunt oculi mei salutare tuum
Quod parasti ante faciem omnium populorum.

Those long eyelashes need a cuticle scissors.

Stroke his forty-year-old face in the halo
Of the wordless ad break that is dawning on him
Slowly with the sound turned down to zero now
In the soft light of the ad for Milk Flake,
The light of the Oil of Olay ad,
Spring water that sparkles until ice is added.

TOUCH WOOD

Some part of me still needs to make the sign of the Cross.
Not so much on my own breastplate in the old way
As a cortège, say, passes in the motorway's slow lane –
From the join of the eyebrows to the bellybutton,
From the bellybutton to the left nipple
And then from the left nipple to the right nipple –
Like the practised incisions of a hospital autopsy.
Thus Mother Power in my Montessori classroom.

Not that at all, though. And not sweet Jesus either
Strung up in a brown study like a colostomy patient
With shitty stuff seeping from his side in sepia;
Or even the pretty Christ on my parents' chimney breast,
Long haired and homosexual, a teenager's hard-on,
Serenely studying my father's masculine buttocks
As a single sperm with my homunculus in it
Shot like a circus cannonball into nineteen fifty-five.

Still something in my life at fifty-plus
Needs to touch wood. Needs, out of the criss-cross,
Out of the double-cross, of my drive to fashion in wood
That slipshod, shedding, dead deciduous place
Where I couldn't tell the forest from the trees,

Couldn't hear birdsong.
                              These went against the grain:
Hardwood hacked from a looted Asian allotment,
The prestige bog-oak of a bourgeois holiday home;
Cash-crop conifers in a sterile industrial unit
And the proletarian slipknots of a rushed-job Brigid's cross.

But not the miniature splints of a cross my daughter made
In the pious aftermath of her first Holy Communion,
Matchstick by glued-on matchstick. Our deal kitchen table
Was a log-jammed landing, a shanty settlement flattened.
She had left the Lucifer heads with the sulphurous smell.

Someday, up in the attic, among the tagged suitcases,
The collapsible tree, the Christmas crib with the rat killer,
It may go up in flames and show me once and for all
Between the fire alarm and the fire extinguisher –
From the site of the migraine to the sink of the navel,
From its dry waterhole to the male waste of a nipple
And across the primate wilderness of the classical torso –
A fireball, a long-haired star, a gate-crashing god.

THE O'CONOR DON SJ

Each morning he would meet the Mathews brothers
At the piggery near Saint Francis Xavier's garden
On their way to serve the half-past seven Masses.
And he would hand them two hard orchard apples,
Lacquered on the wing of his black soutane,
And tell them the Latin for cooker and for pippin
And which was the fruit in the Garden of Eden.
They would sink their teeth in them after Communion
On the pillbox dome of the school Bomb Shelter,
A halfway house between pig swill and Pentecost.

He was Church and State, their own father told them,
Broadswords and breviaries in his blue bloodstream.
Yearly *The Times* would publish his birthday:
'The O'Conor Don, the last descendant
Of the High Kings of Ireland, is today aged —'
When he consecrated, a wolfhound barked twice,
Once for the Host and once for the chalice.
But unless he eloped with a child-bearing bride
To beget a royal republican Don,
His line would end in a limbo forever,
An apple core fed to the prodigal swine.

If the dream of a son made him cry in his sleep
She could drink his tears to become pregnant.
There'd be fruit of her womb then, a kingly priesthood.
No wonder The O'Conor Don SJ
Wandered around the farmyard with his prayer book,
Worrying which kind of a Father he should be;
Yet still finding time for the likes of two brothers
Who would leave this golden autumn for the winter
To marry the filth and the flood like the Doge of Venice
With Jesus stuck on the train tracks of their teeth
And the smell of pig shit in their balaclavas.

They freewheel past me still. It is far down the road.
Desertion, death, and the closed hospital wards.
It is a turning that we turn from in slow motion,
Spellbound by our last sight of the twentieth century
Where Adam blamed Eve and Eve blamed the serpent
And a stray went home on all fours to his family.
Seminaries silent. Churches sold. Priests in prison.
Children impaled. The annihilated father.
And all that harvest fruit preserved now only
As potpourri in a toilet, an atomized windfall.

WATERCOLOUR FOR A WIDOWER
for John

Your wife floats out to sea and is lost
In a real swimsuit, in actual surf.
This, the last birth and the most bitter,
Will taste of salt wind and sand dunes forever
With the medical stench of the ocean's ointment.

Shorelines, outlines, waterlines:
The wet mess they once called the margin.
You stand with your two feet on the ground,
Your toes bedded in hard strand
Like a climber's slowly slipping grip ...

Even Sherpa Tenzing and Hillary
In their face masks and oxygen tanks
Traced at the holy pinnacle
The fossils of starfish in the snow clouds
To go with a jetty twenty miles inland.

Now a granddaughter, an olive branch,
Washes in on a warm wave
From a saltwater uterus
Among girls in white hospital gowns,

Angels with steel oxygen cylinders.

You are the shell of the man you once were.
Put your ear to its aperture.
Listen to the sea that it came from:
Sea of love, sea of loss,
The Aral Sea, the Red Sea, the sea of Atlantis.

As they lift the child and lower her in,
Her fontanel streaming like Mesopotamia,
Will it be any wonder at all,
Salt-of-the-earth man, gilly of the middle ground,
That even your eyes fill up and fulfil

With something strange and saline –
Like the tupperware flask of seawater
I brought home with me from the Mediterranean
And kept on my desk like a skull for a year
Before giving it back to the basin?

FRANCIS OF ASSISI

My bipolar saint, saint of the imaginary,
Whom I love more than the Blessed Virgin Mary
And pray to more than to my loyal Ignatius,
What I want to ask you in your shrewd graciousness
Concerns my manic depression and its mystery:
Is it Brother Catastrophe or is it Sisterly?
(The sibling who carried me in his arms to hospital
Emigrated with good reason to Australia;
And the sisterhood-in-faith that might have visited
Came two years late on the day before my discharge.)
It's a gender-bender not unlike transvestism:
A neutered thing, neither a her nor a him,
Some filthy interim that fools no body,
Hermaphrodite the double Dutch for hell
And lots of circumlocutory doggerel
For the premium files and the files in personnel.
Anafranil and *Lithium* and *Epilim.*
The little vanillas of tranquillity
While my skeleton swells, my skull and crossbones bloat
To balloon like a crash helmet in strong ozone.

But you can tell me, Francis. Male or female?
The wolf came to you with his hang-dog tail,

Why not the werewolf? Look at the pus
Oozing out of my slowcoach paws, the mucus
In the sockets of my eyes. It's been like that
Ever since the Intermediate Certificate,
The time my parents told me *Stop the nonsense*
And go back to bed, boy, though the stairs were melting
In the sweat of my four feet on walkabout.
So is it Sister Stalker or Brother Trauma?
A snake being milked of venom, a fanged vagina
I could die for? You must know the answer.
You took off all your clothes before your father
And walked out of his world. You're cracked forever,
Patron of cissies and the wrecked ecosystem.
With your stuttered paternosters and your rosaries,
Did you grab life by the balls or by the ovaries?
For when I stripped myself in harsher weather,
My auburn ponytail turned to ashen stubble,
Number than Umbria in the wards of Dublin.

MENARCHE

And suddenly there's a gradual silence.
It grows in the space between us like a grand piano,
A Bechstein, too beautiful for my butterfingers,
For your fingerprints among the photo frames.
Or when we speak, not small talk or big talk,
It's as if a Spaniard and an Italian, say,
Were almost understanding every last word
With the large, long-distance gestures of the eyes.

It should be a blessing, a banquet, a bat mitzvah.
I should dance with you again like the Torah
In a moment of visible light
Between past and future, beyond the aim of my retina,
Within a shade of the good colour of blood,
The infrared and the ultraviolet rays
Of the seen and unseen –
My father's penis, my daughter's breasts;
Myself even, the mystic of testicles,
With a belly button like Jesus but no head for heights.

On the feast of day fourteen
We conceived you in speechlessness.
In speechlessness I watched you

Gather your strength between the curious stirrups,
A smashed and soggy redhead,
Angled toward a thigh with no hair, a white hive on it,
As your baptizer's list downsized to Laura.

Another time, I slept. That was day fifteen.
Your mother lay like a Hindu in a handstand,
Her high heels upside down on the faint, flocked
    wallpaper,
To grow you, oval of hope. In the morning,
A heron stood on the chimney pot above us,
Over our heads. Beyond our power of vision.
You could see the neighbours pointing, slowing their cars.
You could hear chart music soaring from the space
    wagons.

The months flow like a movement. Patience and
    passion flow.
I don't write your name and class on your lunchtime
    banana.
The wardrobe ends in wood and not in Narnia.
Now I turn your radio off in the small hours
As you feign deep sleep, that teenage rapid-eye routine.
You move around me warily too
Like the wooden step on the stair that clears its throat

Too audibly after closedown with an atomized
Slipstream of jasmine on the old banister.

When you were small you kissed me on the mouth
Wetly. Nowadays it's the cheek.
Come the piped muzak of hospice care, it'll be my
    forehead.
Please goodness I'll have your chubby, grabbing baby,
Its diaper toppled against my feeding bib,
Spluttering palaver as I put my lips to his/hers,
And knocking my Walkman off so the pillow fills
With a tiny, tinny, immense piano concerto.
Then the whole thing will start again. Our God must
    love it,
Watching our lives as He does in slow, slow motion.
Meanwhile, your bleeding heals me.

SOUNDING THE NAMES
for Pádraig Daly

Let us lift up the 2003 Irish Telephone
Directory like the Gospel book at Mass!
Let the folk group greet it in song!
Let the congregation acclaim it!

Turn it one luminous page at a time
Like the Book of Kells in the college library
From the helmeted child with Down's syndrome
Paddling her waterproof kayak on the cover

Like an aboriginal Firbolg in a log
Canoe, like a grunting Viking oarswoman,
A monk in his giddy coracle, a Norman flotilla,
A Huguenot dinghy at Coliemore Harbour;

All the yawls, ketches, sloops and surfboards
Of our long ascent downstream to this delta
More far-fetched than any raft or hovercraft:
A bobbing, upside-down, biblical ark

With a manifest of names like an altar list
Of the living and their great-grandchildren:

Adelugba, Adeniyi, Adeyemo,
Adkins, Adler, Adlington, Afe,

Advincula, Adye-Curran, Ahern,
Ahmed, Aiken, Alexander, Al Azaid,
Anon, Anonymous, Another!
The A to Z of it, the Alpha and Omega!

But not forgetting the dormitory transports,
Not forgetting my grand-uncle open mouthed
And bare breasted for the male medical orderlies
With their spatulas and stethoscopes

At Ellis Island weeks before Wall Street flooded;
Not forgetting the unfathomable dead
In the closed caterpillar trucks at the dry dock
Whose Trojan cavalry have receded like white horses

To the albs and surplices of the dozy ocean,
To the choir stalls of the lost souls in our bloodstream,
To the salt taste of the lenses in our glasses
And the carte blanche of our last, cleansing Atlantis.

THE COMMUNION OF SAINTS

The true Doomsday Book was not about omens
But about families: *Domus*, the Latin for home.
It was an inventory of hearthstones, a candle Mass.
My daughter drew her granddaddy at his wake
As a black-haired youngster. Crayons cannot do white.
They cannot do newsprint or parchment or papyrus.

My eighty-year-old father is pointing still like Moses
To a sepia of a baby on his chest of drawers.
That is my mother, he says. She fed me for years
    and years.
He tells me: I wish that I had asked you to my wedding.
I show him the hospital scans of his great-grandchildren
The colour of the corpse in the Holy Shroud of Turin.

DOUBLE JEOPARDY

Neither a sheep nor a starling
I flock to the height of my own shedding crown
As a four-footed, down-to-earth astronaut
Who ruminates on the green firmament.

Stars have gone to ground in my skeleton.
Atoms, no less, of the first fierce elements
Glint in my writing hand, in my spinal column,
In the solar plexus where my mother force-fed me.

How can the Greeks in the city endure them,
My pastoral letters of dust clouds and deserts
Or the Temple priests inhabit my Torah,
Its scintillating chasuble of flesh?

I blow between my thumbs on a blade of grass
News from the blue beyond that our weeping faces
And our crying genitals smell of the same,
Of the right, the far-fetched Eastern Mediterranean;

And without an audience or a congregation,
I commune still with my great-grandchildren
Here in my aproned lap where the wind is reading
Page after page an unputdownable paperback.

THE HAND HE HAD TAKEN IN MARRIAGE

Their stitching and unstitching had not been shoddy.
The white line that the serving knife left
Under his watchstrap led back to his body,
Half an individual and half an inmate.

A registrar on the closed ward showed him
The more accurate, the arterial blood flow,
With the corkscrew miniature on his keyring.
You fold the inside wrist like a shadow puppet

While the hand makes a fist. One chaplain fancied it
Like a saint's stigmata; and one woman licked it
In the alcove of an immaculate toilet
While recidivists chain-smoked in the windowless gazebo.

But what of his wife in her sleeveless low-cut top
And the mystery of the hand he had taken in marriage?
The steam burns gone all blonde, the dull dead skin
That will never tan under any sunlamp now,

And an elbow scalded from ovens and barbecues,
Her fingers magnified in a tumbler of water
To ease the ache where she has chanced her arm
And blessed the breadcrumbs at her wedding breakfast?

SYRINGING AN EAR

I offer it to the GP like a waxed vagina
Priggishly, holding my pigtail with my ring finger.

Michaelmas, Hilary, Whit, I'm here not hearing
The uproar of the well for the waterfall's downpour;

Not the ghostwritten skyline of my own vanilla
Suburb or the clinic's Portakabin carpet tiles

Where a sick toddler on a nebulizer
Yawns in my face when he's whooping. Watch his
    mother's mouth

Blow deaf-mute smoke rings from a silent movie
At the bubble captions in the speechless water cooler.

Then the medic's Nicorette breath on my five o'clock
    shadow
Shouts after a parent in Deansgrange graveyard.

I wear cologne for him still and a clean cotton collar;
Mouthwash Listerine thimbles. When we dovetail,

Ditto the doctor. His duty-free aftershave
Reports an odour of airports, inaudible tannoys

While the sound in my left ear clogs, a Wellington boot,
Stone cold, stunned in a sudden pond, a mud plume

Like the mushroom cloud in sepia Second War footage.
Now the other ear is light as a moccasin slipper

Tracking the stickiness of a slug's slow glister
Through the pulverised grass outside, the Jew's harp

Of the hairs in the cashier's nostril at reception,
And the bowl brought forward finally, like a sacrament,

In the kidney shape of an aluminium chalice
With all my greasy sediment, black bits and bobs,

A wake-up call for today's echolocation
Of the broad daylight where I moonlight, wax and wane,

Curetted, irrigated, a canal again
And pierced by the most infrequent frequencies:

The shriek and muzak of this, that, and the other.
First the applause. Then the thunderous audition.

ANXIOUS TO BE HOPEFUL

Life is hard enough without having to.
Only nicotine makes the heart race now,
Not the BBC World Service,
The Medical Missionaries of Mary
Or the Christmas edition of *Readers' Wives*.

You go animal vegetable mineral.
As you clear the car wash at the service station
A spider staggers from the passenger mirror
To work on a jury-rig of her wet, wrecked web;
And the cactus in a basket with builders' cement
Aslant on the outhouse windowsill
Flowers on the last Tuesday of November.
They are not enough, these makeshift signs. But you
    let them.

Your skeleton weighs a ton yet your skull
Is as light-headed as osteoporosis.
Those lithium tablets you take *nocte*
Are pellets of moonshine, pinches of salt,
Marking a pathway back to your body,
To the brain that minds you and reminds you,
In the hard slog of the dogged cogito,

It is not enough that you monologue.

Someday you'll wake with an erection.
The cactus will fruit during a freeze-up,
The spider decommission her net
To starve like a desert anchorite
While a BBC broadcast in Swahili, say,
Memorializes the wives of God.
And the reading wife in bed beside you
Will look up, listening to the bulletin.
She'll be naked again, nude even
Apart from the smut of Ash Wednesday,
No drawstring of a tampon
Dangling between her thighs like a ripcord:
The *femme fatale* from whom you made
A *femme de ménage* in the twenty-first century.

But for one who puts small stones in his mouth
Like those public speakers in the Peloponnese
To practise their outcry clearly;
For one who has breakfasted aghast
On the consolations of breathlessness;
For one who has played with the whole of zero for years
Like a steadfast child with a hoop,
Enough is enough is enough.

NOSTALGIAS

In Greece where I can read road signs
And headlines in the old alphabet
To my little daughter's delight –
Monodromos, say, for cul-de-sac,
And *Exodos* the only way out –
It is Plato who cuts my hair,
Blowing softly on my psoriasis,
While my wife takes a flash photograph;
Aristotle who stamps tickets
At the municipal parking lot,
And Alexander a summer waiter
Who studies earthquake data
And who asks me all about Ireland
While my child is casting her bread
In crumbs to the feeding shoals
Where the sea is clear to the bottom
And a boy is swimming between
The scissor legs of his girlfriend
In the place that they raised the mosaic
Of the dancers joining forces.

Driving up North again,
Weekending with earnest worshippers

In Roman temples, Reform ones,
Criss-crossing this Hebrew province
To broadcast religious services
But sowing no seed at all,
Just like homesick Pausanias
Who catalogued Greek sanctuaries,
Cathedrals of Zeus and Apollo
And the oratories of Demeter,
It is Isaac who serves me water
In a Ballymena pub,
And Ignatius who sells me TCP
In a street that prohibits spirits.
On the hedged roads no way forward,
No way out. When the headlights
Target the road signs, it's always
The godawful, the atrocious names –
Greysteel, Poyntzpass, Omagh,
Kill this, Cull that, Enniskillen –
That swim into the blindness
Like forms of life not seen before
From some deep unmanned submersible.
All you can do is pray,
Gun the motor and touch base:
The smell of the child strapped in the seat,
Fallen forward and sideways, asleep.

STRANDED

Hope and history don't rhyme.
They just alliterate
If you aspirate correctly,
Eliza Doolittle-style.
But the metre is a mantra
Like the billboards on the motorway,
Miles from my route at midnight
Between headlights and cat's eyes
And the signage of two statelets.
The thoughts of it still tranquilize
Like the blindspot of the monstrance
In the Church of the Blessed Sacrament
Where we pray for our daily bread
To be polyunsaturated;
And the slogans of ad campaigns
That flash on stand-alone screens
Give a taste of eternal life:
A *secondaire* in Sicily,
The good orgasm from Guinness,
Resentment and desire
The art of all our business,
The business of all our art.
History hoped for a bonus.

That Mass is over. Go in pieces
To love and serve a lasting chrysalis,
Defiled by our own virtues
And the purity of our vices,
Our cultural Pax Penicillin
All crisis and no Christ Jesus.

But the murderers in their gowns
Who cannibalized his body
In the black mass of atrocity,
The Eucharist of the cockroach,
Wave their honorary doctorates
At an uptown photoshoot –
Their capped and crowned teeth flossed
To gloss and to gloss over –
On their way to the Parliament
Where politicians stress
Peace and reconcilement
Who have walked out on their missus,
Leaving the *femmes de ménage*
For the *femmes fatales'* wet kisses,
The kitchen sink for a pink oasis
That dissolves into the desert.
And the meek will inherit the earth
As they always do and have done,

The geological paydirt
Of a cemetery whose janitors
In an equal, ecumenist's land
Beyond Lambeg drums and *feiseanna*
And the birdless columbarium –
And beyond the beyond of myself
With my Carmelite in one fist
And my bulletpoints in the other –
Will be Muslims from Bangladesh
Who believe in the Virgin birth,
In the fruit that falls in her lap
And her steaming, stable placenta.

A VICTIM OF THE TROUBLES

I want to pretend you were brought up
In a small house, say, in Jerusalem Street;
Went partying in Damascus Road
To be burned with a blowtorch in Joy or Hope.

It would make just the perfect finishing poem
For a joint Arts Council breakaway week
Touring to Berkeley or Petersburg even.
It would say that *I bleed. I do not shed blood.*

None of this posthumous sadness is lost on me
For I am the alias of the Lord Jesus.
And maybe a Jewish sophomore auditing
Great Western Works (2B: Advanced Course)

Will hopefully go down on me after
Or whip my penis with her black plait
In a studio loft in the faculty ghetto
Where small change fills the charity fountain

With pennies from heavenly conference centres,
Kopecks and shekels, the tokens for trolleys.
It is part-trash. It is one hundred per cent,

The dash from cut-and-thrust to cut-and-paste.

So I want to pretend that you were *et cetera*,
For who can imagine what really happened?
No Microsoft of mine will ever
Lengthen your lifetime or shorten your parents'.

Joy, Jerusalem, Hope, Damascus,
Neither the Good Book nor the *Golden Pages*;
Just the dry lining, the damp-proof beauty board
Where you have been stalked and shadowed for ages.

DEATH AND THE MAIDEN MATHEWS

At seventeen he could think only of death,
Inhaled it like the stain on a girlfriend's underwear,
Breathing the beautiful detail of his abolition
In the period whiff of a saline *Odyssey*.
At the hospital where he worked as a dog's body
He found any excuse to promenade the morgue
Like Elgin among his marbles in the British Museum.

Forty years on, more or less, and biodegradable,
He takes his tablets in multivitamin peppermint.
The growth between his legs is beyond Viagra
And only the mobile throbs. It is always on silent.
Down Paradise beach on the hetero side of Mykonos
He roams like David Attenborough, effeminate, horny,
To commune with the sea lion couplings under both
    species.

THE HONOURS SYSTEM

Primo Levi embodied the best in our human nature
Et cetera. Likewise the great man Elie Wiesel
Doing Torah Talmud now with the sophomores at
    Bologna
Or shepherding Oprah Winfrey down the selection ramp.
They had both figured in the death camps, both had
    transfigured them.
All the grey men with their glasses on who are interviewed
In front of their paperback bookshelves for a documentary
    pogrom
Salute them. Me too, the solitary inmate of my barbed-
    wire body.
Like an Early Christian believer who never saw Jesus
    in person
But afterwards met an apostle, I stand as a witness to
    these witnesses.

But what about Doctor Ruth who survived Auschwitz
    as well?
She taught me all I know about the prostate gland,
    its pleasures,
The clitoris, rear entry, and that beautiful banana enema.
She chuckles and the beast turns over on its back. She soars

Into the Milky Way like the cow in a Chagall painting.
    To her,
The good rabbi of bedlam, a contemplative nun
Of our strict, intrinsic life, a Sufi of sweat and fever,
Swami of all our mucous membrane, yogi of the orgasm,
Who dances with her two feet on the ground against the
    airborne fanatics,
Be honour and glory too.

TENEBRAE

Their holiest Communion was manic depression,
The bypassed password for bipolarity;
That and a sort of idolatry of the latrine;

Her own psychosis in the drawing-room downstairs
Being the longest menopause on record,
Seasons obsessing under the same ceiling rose.

What were those white prescription pills in the card table
That her children used for poker chips, for Pontoon?
Who in the world was her wall-fallen father

Waiting for hours downstairs with the indoor help
While her nails dried in the pose of a priest's blessing
At the dressing-mirror's Netherlandish triptych?

And who was that elderly child
She checked in the small hours in his counterfeit coma,
His dangerous diaries kept in Greek and pidgin?

One night they fought under overhead light on a landing.
He in his brother's stapled pyjama bottoms,
She in a slip and ludicrous pompom socks:

After she'd pummelled his chest with her fists,
He cradled her waist with his wrists as she cried
Snot and sputum on a pink candlewick bedspread.

It was the closest they'd ever come.
She weeping with whatever it was that wept her,
Him and his mantras. *Abba. Abattoir. Toi.*

And the next time he'd sidle beside her cot
Was a fin-de-siècle scene, sick in a psychiatric
Cubicle packed with the brood-mare brides of her era.

There, in his hardness of heart, he made mental notes,
Not knowing his own clothes would be whisked from
    him later
By a nurse who mistook his surname for his Christian.

Hers was a botched finale, his was a botched beginning.
So I study my daughters. I discern them daily,
Half the monk Mendel and half a Doctor Mengele.

I'd spring you into purgatory if I could, ma'am.
It says in some epistle we can all be Trojans.
Creeds tell us too one descended to the dead.

Do as much for me so and my two descendants.

Lift up your eyes to me like the mother of Odysseus.

Kiss like a grandchild would. Do not eat the face off me.

BASTILLE DAY

With a pikestaff or a musket or whatever
The poor of Paris threw in the air like caps,
Let me burst into my own Bastille wherever
Masonry offers a gap.

Let me find no sentries in the courtyard,
No one to prevent my picking the lock
Of the keyhole at the one solidly mortared
Occupied cell in the block.

Inside there's a man. Aged, arthritic,
He blinks in the sudden glare of the lantern.
The beard on his chest unravels like knitting
As he kneels to my tantrum.

'Are you that father?' I ask him, 'whose language
Was a glance of menace, a cold word spoken
To browbeat?' And he: 'How can you gauge
A life that was broken

Before it began? You remember the shot
Of myself as a seven-year-old with a pop gun?
Did you truly imagine my eyes to be shut

Tightly because of the sun?

And who do you think had been holding the camera
As I stood to attention among the hydrangeas,
Waiting his signal to enter the era
Of five-year plans and Falangists?

What have I done to merit your anger?
I too was an orphan.' Now, shoulder to shoulder,
We stand in a circle of pity and danger,
And his face is the image of mine, only older.

STRICTLY NO POETRY

In the *Writers' & Artists' Yearbook*
Under London Literary Agents
The slanted print said: *Strictly No Poetry*.

Like the *Strictly No Irish Wanted*
Of my great-granduncle's last months
In the Minnesota dustbowl he planted,

Gagging on what had once been dear to him,
All farmed and gorgeous green in the ordnance survey
When he gawped at it in a former era

Before the strong and silent movies
Opened their mouths and talked in plain American.
The sounds of my family tonight –

Latino hits on *MTV*, Homer
Simpson and the shock jocks on kitchen radio –
Blow my tercets back in my face forever too;

And who am I in midlife to deny
The high harmonica on the set does move me
More than Bach's *Mass in B Minor* did

Or that anything I could write for my wife
Is less than the day's finessed witch-finding
In those flammable, early-edition tabloids?

Yet I summon my patron saint to my side
(She's a teenage hospice hairdresser,
Chaplain of no diplomas yet) to bless

My heritage of Hiberno-Latin,
Bog-standard broad and slender with slender,
Newsprint alongside fresh papyrus.

Thomas Edison took
Three thousand tries to find himself
The right form for his light filament –

Gold, silver, bronze,
Copper, tin, flint; then a waxed thread
To guide him through the labyrinth.

Thus my great-granduncle Tom's
Aged aplomb at the cine-camera stage,
Home to a grandniece who frowned like his mammy.

The trimeter still said: *Strictly No Poetry.*

Not even my metaphorical wet dreams,
My puberty's pious ejaculations,

Or the hushed Hail Marys I was versed in then.
That mid-West dust I spoke of has settled
Like pollen in the pleats of my eyelids,

In the true grit of actual scarcity.
And whose twisters are writhing now like a stylus
For better and worse through my own pillar of cloud?

EUCHARIST AT THE FULL MOON

There's nothing new under the sun
But this, our moon's original darkness:
Homosexual men cruising, God bless them,
At the Papal Cross in the Phoenix Park,

And debutantes on Grand Canal dock
With their espadrilles in Marc Jacob bags,
Or a Malaysian medical student perhaps
Tasting his first alcopop lips in Europe;

And the whiff of my wife beside me in the bed,
That we have made and must lie upon truly,
Her scent of surf and turf on the wet duvet.
Dawn is about to happen here overnight.

That metal secateurs for any intruder
Hits the floor with the cold hot-water bottle
And the manila folder from Human Resources
While the child in the cot cries: 'Daddy, sky is back!'

And my own brown blood on the lit ceiling rose
From a kamikaze mosquito last August
Passes over our singular first-person plural.

April's still by far the best theology

In a lunatic calendar that can never
Be quite sure how to date the West's Easter:
Tonight's vigil could be Ash Wednesday next year,
Good Friday the Annunciation, even.

Under a full moon, its rolled futon,
The whole world may be going to Holy
Communion under both species,
The host itself a Corpus Christi planet

Placid behind the helmeted red bricks. How its halo
Ghosts our fake-tan torso in a whitewash
Over a silent fraction of moist toast,
Breakfast in bed, the midnight's slow breadline.

COURTSHIP

Ours was an old-style Irish romance,
A slow advance from head to haunch.
My hand in your page-boy fringe the first month,
Tongues of fire through the melting train tracks.

An autumn after our first meeting,
You unburdened your burgundy bolero;
The two breasts greeted and given pet names,
Nipples nesting in fashionable muslin.

Then the warm slope of the small of your back,
My asylum, the unsurpassable place;
And at last the liquid entrance in,
All Latin it was and chanted pidgin.

Not to mention the like of your lap, lady:
No article from anatomy texts,
But a human compact that,
A landscape of actual flesh and bloodshed.

If, after thirty-five years, I could bear
To reprise my plodding nomad in mono,
I would not colonize the wry armpit,

Navel or vulva. Strong small partner,

Asleep in a queen-size bed in streetlight,
Your face is haloed in the glow of an iPhone.
Nothing I have done to it so far shows
The closed folding doors, the corkscrew stairwell,

Yet twice now since the new term started,
I have watched the mask grow backwards quickly
To before there were crowns or a first lip wax,
Eyeshadow, the little moustache of tears.

Only your two feet fight free of the duvet.
They have corpsed; they are beyond chiropody,
Washed and rubbed raw and scraped with scissors
For no priest's hand towel on Holy Thursday.

UNDERGROUND

A thousand days. One night. Illness to illness.
Where they were building the lift at the new locked ward
A sign on the scaffold read in Irish and English:
We apologise for the noise of reconstruction.

In the cafeteria with the plastic cutlery
Lives could be borne if only they were meaningless.
I think my father said that. Or did he say
He had been as unhappy as me and had always hidden it?

For a thousand days I said nothing to anyone, so,
But *Please* and *Thank you. Thank you very much.*
It was like being lost again in the Paris Metro
At the age of ten, knowing only *S'il vous plaît, monsieur,*

And *Merci, madame,* among the strange, swaying bottoms,
Perfume and shrieks and the bobsleigh sickness starting.
Shrill capitals on the tunnel curves italicized
Invalids Only, Invalids Only, Invalids. Up

In the little republic of the sun my host family
Were photographing each other with Instamatics
By the elm tree in the Irish College courtyard. But here,

Deeper than cells and sewers, deeper than septic tanks,

Saints I had never heard of mispronounced sentence.
Kilometres above me, place names opened like orchards.
The long-haired women sat in their short skirts, scowling,
With those terrible white triangles staring back at me.

When I had slotted my small French change inside
     my shoes,
I cleaned my glasses with the end of my new school tie
And stood up straight at last as the seats shot into
     darkness.
Nobody spoke one word. And I begged their pardon.

TWO THEATRES

for Robin at Hogmanay

'... jewgreek meets greekjew ...'

From a locked ward in one state, intensive care in another,
The same solstice dragged us to a hospital window
In cotton tops as lightweight as linen beachwear.
My brain had a mind of its own. You were out of
    your body.

And this is where we bypassed, friend. This was the first
Call, the first contact, the first correspondence.
A surgeon lifted your heart from the cage of your chest
As obstetrically as a Caesar section

While I woke among electrodes in a cot bed
To the taste of anaesthetic, old chocolate liqueur,
Like the bad breath of the fast before Communion
And our fathers there at the far end growing farther.

Your heart's in the right place now, the left of centre,
Like the woman that Yahweh dreamed up from a rib.
You can milk dissolving stitches, the male nipple,
The cheloid scar underneath Eliot's waistcoat;

And I'll prompt my fontanel into a tonsure too.
My scripts will be salt of the earth for the next thirty years,
A wise old owl, in fact, instead of Pallas Athena
Impregnating my temple like a Marian grotto.

CHOPSTICKS IN DRY DOCK

Tomorrow a new concerto, tomorrow
The gloves applauding like a flock of seabirds.

Tomorrow a virtuoso performance,
Despair of even the ambidextrous.

Tomorrow a heartfelt lecture on
The Day's Practice as the Day's Perfection.

But today, this midwinter morning in June,
The first phrase of a tune called Chopsticks.

My two legs dangle in pins and needles
From the swivel stool at the slanted piano;

My hands in hiding. In the hospital grounds
Egg is trickling from the magpie's corkscrew,

Basil from the barber-pole caterpillar.
Yet the white keys and the black keys calm me,

The cigarette finger that a daughter once sucked
And the ring finger the secateurs snapped.

Yet the first phrase of a tune called *Chopsticks*
Is shushing the programme notes of an opus

Called future perfect, not perfect future,
Of *pentimenti* that are pentatonic.

The four walls weep. My holiday schnorkel
Mists on the antlers of the hall's old hatstand

And the horsefly floating on the big bay window
Dies in the focus of its Mayday emergence

When red-hot pokers teemed at the boathouse
With the genital scent of stock and night jasmine.

For the first phrase of that tune called *Chopsticks*
Is rising and setting, a wetness, a freshet,

To comfort the water tank caulked in the attic
Which will creak in due course like the clinkers of a hull,

Remembering the sole lunacy of the moon,
The kingdom of currents, a monsoon empire.

CHRISTMAS DAY

I.

My children kneel at the fire
In an odour of forest.
The Wizard of Oz on the set,
Snow White on box cassette.

Somewhere but far away
Afterbirth may be steaming
Under a burnt-out bus shelter
In Bosnian-minus temperatures.

We've sheltered here all day
Since we left our card in the manger
Where the priest had woken Santa
On a mobile phone from the altar.

Now we can watch the films
As the kindling flames with a roar
And be tense with annoyance if
The flap on the letterbox lifts

To a whistle at the door

Just when the singing Princess is hand-
Wringing dormitory gingham
Or the Wicked Witch of the North

Dwindles in front of Dorothy.
Somewhere but far away
A woman in labour budges
Another red inch of skull

In a twitching shawl of horseflies
Under an ad for Coke.
But I am taking tablets
For thoughts that are ruminations –

They handsel me like pebbles,
Leading me back where I stood
With my two daughters in firelight
And the phantom reek of pinewood.

2.

Somewhere but far away,
In the lost last century,
From shuls and prep schools and shtetls
And yeshivas and yacht clubs'

Cadet classes, Yiddish kids
Crowd to the nickel'n'dime
Cinemas of Llov, Lublin,
Of Luxembourg, Athens, Rome –

All the fairy-tale motherland
Milestones from the Brothers Grimm
Before the grim brotherhood.
And they laugh and they cry out loud

At *Snow White* and *The Wizard of Oz*.
Inexhaustible ambulances
Have opened their doors already
To the dwarves of Greater Germany.

The handicapped heartbroken
Stare at the red-brick road that rises:
The Strawman drenched in paraffin
For his mental impediment,

The Tin Man stripped for metal
Because he could not be heartless,
The Lion skinned as a footstool
For the gallantry of his gentleness;

And the children then. The lost
Commonwealth of Walt Disney;
The *Juden* of garlanded wreaths.
They sit in raptures at ovens

Where no unleavened breadloaves
Steam in the stench of a pine plantation,
Its vast choir stall of Christmas trees,
At a mass grave. At the grave of the Mass.

Firelight streams from the watchtowers,
Stars, the proscenium arch,
Where the torches of uniformed men
Usher them through the dark parterre.

And does even one of them hide in the gods,
A clubfoot, while the curtains close,
For the last phrase of the credits' shrill
Roll call fading under the houselights?

A PENGUIN LIBRARY

It's the closest you can come to autobiography:
The paperbacks and hardbacks on your pine bookshelf,
Castrato arias; a countertenor's octave.

The Gospels in Greek. Althusser. Magical Realism.
You want so much to belong. You belong to the wanting.
They began as woodland once and they end as Ikea

Eco-friendly coffins four brothers hammered together
The year the Sabras looted the camp at Chatila
In the smoke of the last of the cedars of Lebanon.

Our kids are far too happy to be reading this
Philistine rant by a pseudo-Palestinian.
Their dormers look the other way, out on the raining,

And the plasma TV blazes like a chimney breast.
What was it I was reading? Something that spoke to me
In the whiff of wife and the diesel of the street.

When I slipped my finger inside you, the paper
   cuts stung.
On our marriage night of real flesh and bloodshed

My thesis on the Ulster poets blocked

A hairline hole in the floor where a lookalike white lab
Mouse of the old sort before these cursor computers
Thirsted for water, and could not be sourced.

THIS IS ILLYRIA, LADY

Sooner or later I shall let them in,
Dark and the conifers also.
I shall lay their threshold like a table first:
A bread loaf shallow as a ballet shoe
And the glassy Eucharist of my own thirst.

Then will be all my Christmases, so:
The massed, industrial pines
That host no solstice for atrocity –
Dormitories of stirrup and gas mask! –
Where backpackers squat now to piss quietly.

Sooner or later I shall have to let them,
Dark and the conifers too.
Meticulous insect, moon of my thumbnail,
And the needles' tiny toilet-bowl scent
Like the whiff of a long-lost broadleaf library

That would have shown me the wood from the trees,
The weatherboard of the root-work's wicker
At last; sterility of the evergreen;
And the footfall of one walkabout, static
Well within earshot, like a wafer's fraction.

ADAM'S ENLIGHTENMENT

Granted it came as something of a shock
To be shown the door in a stony silence,
I was not put out. I had made provision.

True, for a time I could only stare,
Moving slowly as if through water
And whistling to keep my body in business.

Yet it ended well when the cattle waded,
Welcoming, smelly, towards my encampment
To be milked clean, to be manhandled.

In a maiden brainstorm I then invented
Firelighters, fishing hooks,
And a rudimentary method of blaming

Somebody else for my own misconduct,
While a trial five-year plan includes
Facsimiles in a brood of children

Plus any amount of adjectives
To ensure that the view from my picture window
Will never leave me lost for words:

What I once called yokes I now call names.
You may quote me on this. I am thrilled silly
To have finished at last with the other fellow,

My godfather of gardening fame,
And I wash my hands of his shitty, seignorial
'Never mind me, I'm one of you' nonsense.

Though I have it on highest authority
That he misses me, there is no going back.
I draw the line at every horizon:

The world I want is what lies about me,
What crops up where you least expect it
In a surplus bigger than barns can harvest,

And slap, bang in the middle there's me,
A master of ceremonies, a centre of gravity,
Braincells in a prism of sunlight.

And what of the angel looking daggers
At Eden's doorway, his brandished sword's
Acetylene tip wagged back and forth?

It moved to the back of beyond out there,

Circling me at a distance. It does still,
As plain as daylight from dawn to dusk.

Noblesse oblige. I take it lying down
On the flat of my back and watch it work
Wonders, tugging the barley by its ears,

Making the apples chubby, the cabbage
Sprawl as if it had a right to be there.
It touches even me when I let it. My forehead

Darkens beneath it to a brown study
While my shadow goes to enormous lengths
To take in as much ground as it can.

So I can state categorically and for now
That I am happy, that I am about
To imagine a new God for myself. Already

I am kicking several ideas around.
I think I shall make a fist of my hands
And the wife's face too, with or without tears.

HOME ECONOMICS

What we used to call domestic science
In the Esperanto of the day before yesterday.
Sitting in saffron, sort of, and humming *home*
Under the photographs over the fireplace –

Me in Auschwitz, you in Tiananmen Square –
And the managed forests of our bookshelves
Where you can't see the wood for the trees,
All cash-crop conifers and no birdsong.

We need classics, yes. We need trash too,
Says Bernard Shaw, two down and one across.
So today I set aside Ovid the divo
For more of Wolf News and the Hitler Channel.

These days the nights have gone without saying,
These nights the days speak for themselves:
Their pluck, their pizzicato drizzle
Like the static of those Cycladic crickets

Where the first of our two children started
A rapid slippage to Babylon: bibs,
Baby talk and the good Ottoman

Empire of a couple of tenured couch potatoes

Who will watch the grim Rwandan drama
Or was it Burundi in that Indian summer
You went from the scent of lime and mandarin
To the odour, lady, of Pomegranate Noir?

LATE ENTRY IN THE BOOK

There will be dormitories, a safe place set apart
For those who started bravely but finished second,
A sanctuary for the runners-up
Whose only trophy was the fall on camera;
A shrine for the semi-finalists
With their silver-plated plaques and nickel shields;
An ashram for the posthumous in their prime.
The lives they followed were not lives they led.
They lived in second place to their loved rivals,
Survived in second place to their loathed role models.
Deafly the half-lives vie.

Neither Mercedes nor Rolls shall devote this grotto
But Benz and his mirror Royce
And the second transplant patient to take fresh heart
From the pioneering surgery of Christian Barnard.
The sequel to the wedding feast at Cana
Shall be first and foremost in its liturgies
With a sad Sephardic bride, her grandfather groom
And the sediment turning to soot in the potty carafes
While the karaoke continues wine into water.
A girlfriend's second miscarriage that April morning,
Which was neither as traumatic as the first omen

Nor as final as the last, a catacomb creche,
Shall see her a Paraclete yet of the pre-natal clinics.

Under its rainforest canopy like a hospital
Will be found the hundred chiropodists of Nagasaki
And those who died of obesity in Herzegovina
Instead of in battle in Bosnia the same fortnight.
The second scientist to have thought of the double helix,
Survival of the fittest and the blood's circulation,
Will escort the Number Two Northern hunger striker
    who starved
Through the last lingering second thoughts of his mother,
And accompany too the second love of my life
Who was my wife, my one and only, the second I saw her
In the swapshop skirt that would give me many erections,
Searching a second-hand stall for my copycat paperbacks.

There have been so many persons I did not put first,
Persons shortlisted although they were second to none.
The last shall be first, says the second such Gospel, but
    what of the Vices?
Shadow me then as I follow in their shoes,
A rung at a time, like the second man on the moon,
Who climbed down the long stepladder of the lunar
    module

To find at his feet the ground he was standing on
And somebody else's footprints in every direction.

NEW YEAR'S RESOLUTION
i.m. Dennis O'Driscoll

A fair-trade cent on each and every latte
(Decaf, of course) for our twinned Honduran family;
My bit, such as it is, for the thirsty planet:
The hot tap turned off tightly while I mouthwash.

Plus the sheer bad manners of more poetry
Breathing through my cold sores wherever I go
And saving the artisan bread through the sorbet course
For that adulterous mallard from the Dodder falls

Who turns up April Fool's Day with his biddies
Where the pond has gone to ground in the Radio Centre.
More music, much less talk, in other words,
Same as the slogan on the pre-set station, Q something,

A moment of G minor worthy of Abba
Or a line from the early Bee Gees, a countertenor's cry.
Which would be asking for too much, much too late.
But writing more lightly, drinking more heavily, Dennis,

And dancing with the alcohol molecule
The way Miss Piggy danced with Rudolf Nureyev,

Forgetting for a while the state of my underwear:
Togs soaked in the North Atlantic under a rented tux.

And the letters AMDG written in full DayGlo
At every page turn, lemon, lavender, blue,
Over the scatty Latin and the bungled algebra, yes,
And the thought of you.

A VALENTINE FOR ASH WEDNESDAY
after Chaucer's Parlez-Vous of Birds

Its life so brief, its art long in the learning,
Its shock so cutting and its outcome doubtful,
Those dreadful pangs of pleasure when we're yearning –
This is what Love's about. Love's a right mouthful.
Love leaves me breathless or is it more like winded?
In a word: sore. And when I think about it
I can't be sure whether it's worth my spouting.

Not that I've first-hand knowledge – only wet dreams –
Of how passion repays us or pays us back.
Now and again I've glanced at magazines.
You know the sort of masochistic trash
Where the guy's on all fours, the girl's a dominatrix,
And love's a stroke of fortune. Bottoms up!
Even the purest love is symptomatic.

You think I stopped at centrefolds? I didn't.
I've studied paperbacks too from the Pelican Library.
Why am I telling you this? Because a hidden
History fell from my bookshelf full of breviaries
Only the other day, and I was intrigued
By its microscopic print, by its silverfish.

I sat there reading till my backside stiffened.

There's a true saying I saw somewhere or other
About the fields at harvest time, *et cetera*,
How ripeness happens at God's good speed, no bother;
And books are the same. Dumas or Derrida,
They open to disclose us. Now or not quite yet,
The fullness of time will bring us to a text
That fills us with the sweetness of a sacrament.

Ditto with me. The book. It was Cicero's
Dreamtime of Scipio. The blurb says it best.
'Dante without the *Purgatorio*!
It makes a hell of heaven, a heaven of hell! Sex
Can never be the same again! Superb! Shortlisted!'
Basically it's been out of print for ages,
So bear with me. I'll summarize its pages.

It kicks off with one Scipio's arrival
In Africa BC where he meets a Masinissa.
They are sort of role-models cum real rivals
And the whole day passes in reminiscence
And a kind of heated hetero karaoke.
Then they go to bed. Scipio sleeps. He dreams.
His most illustrious ancestor invades his REM,

The ghost of the great General Africanus
Who sacked the city of Carthage – Hannibal's, Hippo's –
He sounds more of a prophet than proconsul
As he prophesies now his future life to Scipio,
A man who imagined that an ignoramus
Who loves the world God made can teach monsignors
The true itinerary of the magi's star.

So Scipio plucks his courage up. 'Do the dead survive?
Is there any truth to the Resurrection story?'
And Africanus says: 'They are alive.
Their sufferings are a part of ancient history.
They thrive because their faith was beyond belief.
Lumpen and prolish, they were God's own leaven.
What we call starlight is their host of heaven.'

The shade showed him the plotline: our little earth
Diminutive and green as any olive,
The constellations in a whitening blizzard
And the intergalactic holes that Hawking speaks of.
The music of the spheres is a girlfriend's fart,
Scipio muttered to himself. Why not hallow
The real stars from Hollywood we follow?

But Africanus urged him: 'Life is awful.

The more you love, the more you're vulnerable.
Eros or agape, it all ends in a muddle.
Besides, who can cry halt to Armageddon?
The time is fast approaching when the huddled
Masses of interstellar space will vanish
Along with the pretensions of our planet.'

So Scipio asked him: 'What am I to do
To save my soul then if I can't save my skin?'
And Africanus: 'No drink, no dope, no Voodoo.
Study the theology of liberation.
God made you immortal and He meant to.
Don't be led by the nose or by the penis.
Celibacy is the body's work of genius.

As for the others, dykes and drag-show queens,
Priapic clerics, sickos and transsexuals,
They are utterly fucked as far as I can see.
They'll serve time in eternity, balls or no balls,
Orbiting our Paradise purgatorially
Until they're sorry, until they've learned their lesson,
When bygones are bygones, and they get remission.'

My bedside reading faded. Phut. The night-world
Woke up the free, rested the working, animals.

On beds everywhere babes with attitude curled.
My book blackened and went out like a candle
At the thought of the strong scent of their genitals.
I hadn't peace of mind because I lacked some
Nice alpha-female for a piece of action.

My flesh was willing but my spirit wobbled,
Bushed as a bookworm should be after reading
An Eng. Lit. classic of the kind I'd gobbled.
I drowsed. I dozed. Was fast asleep and dreaming;
And in that dream the figure from mythology,
Scipio's phantom forebear Africanus
Pulled at the cotton sleeve of my pajamas.

It might have been my id. My own unconscious.
The predator takes a sleeping pill and, presto,
He's salivating over the au pair's haunches;
The barrister revisits verbal brio,
The cabbie's in the car wash at the Esso.
And the dying child in the hospital imagines
Neapolitan ice cream on her crusted tongue.

Whether I'd speed-read or he'd summoned me
I've no idea. He was as large as life,
In technicolour flesh and blood. Not funny.

What was at stake in this was my survival.
But then he said: 'You're my revivalist.
The paper cuts and page turns of your study
Merit reciprocal interest from Yours Truly.'

I prayed: 'Hail, Holy Queen, Mother of Mercies,
Hail, my life, my sweetness, and my hope as well,
If this is a dream, help me to interpret it.
If real, let me run like the hammers of hell
And I'll decorate your statue in the church
Where the dust has settled like pollen.' Think I'm farcical?
Trust in the Virgin. She's the definite article.

She knows I'll sleep with Martha and with Mary.
She knows I'm not selective or selected,
Let alone the *Complete Works* in a posh box set.
I am promiscuous. I am scary. I am all over the thing,
In love-hate with the nakedness underneath nudity:
The soot on your forehead, lady, and the tampon's
    drawstring
On this Ash Wednesday that is Saint Valentine's morning.

Acknowledgments

Irish Pages, Poetry Ireland, Temenos, Irish Independent, The Irish Times, The Stony Thursday Book, Southword, The Wake Forest Series of Irish Poetry and RTÉ Radio 1.